Earth Matters

TRASH MAGIC

A Book about Recycling a Plastic Bottle

by Angie Lepetit

Content Consultant:
Tom Fitz, PhD
Associate Professor of Geoscience
Northland College
Ashland, Wisconsin

CAPSTONE PRESS
a capstone imprint

Gulp! It's easy to grab a bottle of water, juice, or soda when you are thirsty. But where do all those bottles come from? And why is it so important to recycle them? **Let's find out!**

To make a plastic bottle, you start with oil—a dark, sticky fossil fuel. Machines called oil rigs drill for oil deep in the earth. Long, strawlike pipes suck the oil out of the ground.

4

Oil is amazing stuff. It can be made into fuel, used to make roads, or melted into plastic. **But drilling for oil can be dangerous.**

If the rig breaks or the oil
spills, the oil can easily catch fire.
Plus, oil sticks to almost everything
it touches—rocks, plants,
and animals. It can kill
living things.

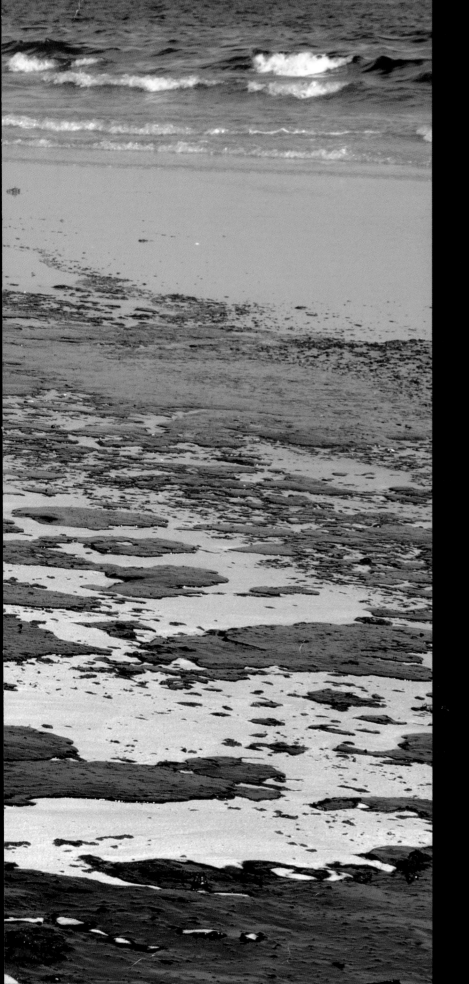

Geologists help oil companies find the safest places to drill for oil. **They try to protect the land, animals, and people that live near the oil rig.**

Making plastic from oil takes a lot of work. First, the oil must be cleaned and heated. When it's really hot, chemicals are added, and the oil thickens. **As it cools, the oil turns into little crumbs called raw plastic.**

Raw plastic doesn't look like much. That's because it needs to get heated again. The crumbs melt together, and more chemicals are added. As the new plastic cools, it becomes stretchy. **Blow air into the stretchy plastic, and you have a bottle!**

Some bottles get filled with milk. Other bottles get filled with water, juice, or soda. The filled bottles are shipped to stores everywhere for us to buy. **What a process!**

It takes a lot of work and natural resources to make a plastic bottle, and millions are used every day. It's too bad not all of them get recycled. Some get tossed to the roadside as litter. Others end up in the ocean. **Even more are put in the garbage and dumped in landfills.**

Here's the problem—plastic does not easily fall apart.

Remember the chemicals used to make the plastic?

It takes hundreds of years for them to leave the bottles.

Once they do, the chemicals soak into the ground.

They can get into our water, which is not safe.

Drinking these chemicals makes you sick.

There's another reason to recycle plastic bottles. Do you remember what dark and sticky liquid makes plastic? That's right: oil. And where does oil come from? Right again: the ground. **If we use oil too fast, we could run out.**

So what can you do with an empty plastic bottle? You could wash it and reuse it. Or you could recycle it. If you want to recycle the bottle, place the bottle in a recycling bin. It's that easy!

Trucks pick up the bottles in the recycling bin. **Off they go to a recycling center.**

At a recycling center, the bottles get sorted. There are signs and numbers on the bottoms of bottles. These tell workers how to group them. The sorted plastic is crushed into large cubes.

After the plastic gets crushed, it is sent to a factory. It gets chopped into flakes and melted. **When the plastic gets stretchy, it is made into something new.**

Recycled plastic often looks like new plastic. It can be made into toys, new bottles, or even slides! Look for recycled plastic at the store. Buying recycled products closes the recycling loop.

Recycled plastic
goes from a store to
you, to a recycling bin, to a
recycling center, to a factory, and back to
a store. **The plastic travels around and around
the same places, like a loop—a recycling loop!**

The recycling loop helps keeps Earth healthy. Less oil is taken from the ground. More animals and plants can keep their homes. Less garbage builds up, and fewer chemicals enter the soil and water.

Let's be mindful about what we use and where it comes from. And let's always remember to recycle. **Earth matters!**

Reused Rumba Shakers

Plastic bottles are great for crafts. Here's a fun craft for you to try—the Reused Rumba Shaker!

You will need:

1 plastic drinking bottle, label removed

dry beans, rice, pasta, or stones

masking tape

markers

Instructions:

1. Fill the clean plastic drinking bottle half full with the dry beans, rice, pasta, or stones. Screw on the cap.

2. Secure the cap with masking tape, and wrap the bottle with masking tape.

3. Use the markers to decorate the bottle.

4. Shake, rattle, and rumba. Have fun!

Glossary

chemical—substances made by or used in chemistry

factory—a building where things like plastic bottles are made in large numbers

fossil fuel—a natural fuel formed from the remains of plants and animals; coal, oil, and natural gas are fossil fuels

fuel—something that is used for energy

geologist—a scientist who studies rocks and the earth

landfill—an area of land where garbage is buried or dumped

liquid—a wet substance that you can pour, such as water

natural resource—something in nature that people use, such as coal, trees, and oil

oil rig—a machine that pulls oil from deep in the earth

process—the actions taken to create something

recycle—to make used items into new products; people can recycle items such as rubber, glass, plastic, and aluminum

soil—dirt

Read More

Fix, Alexandra. *Plastic*. Reduce, Reuse, Recycle. Chicago: Heinemann Library, 2008.

Nunn, Daniel. *Plastic.* From Trash to Treasures. Chicago: Heinemann Library, 2012.

Parr, Todd. *The EARTH Book*. New York: Little, Brown Books for Young Readers, 2009.

Persad, Sabbithry. *Where Do Recyclable Materials Go?* Garbology Kids. Orlando: Ecoadventures, 2011.

Internet Sites

FactHound offers a safe, fun way to find Internet sites related to this book. All of the sites on FactHound have been researched by our staff.

Here's all you do:

Visit *www.facthound.com*

Type in this code: 9781620650493

 Check out projects, games and lots more at
www.capstonekids.com

Index

chemicals, 8, 10, 17, 26

dangers, 5, 6, 17

drilling, 5

fossil fuels, 4

geologists, 7

heating, 8, 10

landfills, 15

litter, 15

melting, 5, 22

natural resources, 15

oil, 4, 5, 6, 7, 8, 18, 26

oil rigs, 4, 6, 7

oil spills, 6

protecting, 7

raw plastic, 8, 10

recycled plastic, 23, 24, 25

recycling bins, 20, 25, 32

recycling centers, 21, 22, 25

recycling loop, 24, 25, 26

sorting, 22

A+ Books are published by Capstone Press,
1710 Roe Crest Drive, North Mankato, Minnesota 56003
www.capstonepub.com

Library of Congress Cataloging-in-Publication Data
The Cataloging-in-Publication information is on file with the Library of Congress.
ISBN: 978-1-62065-049-3 (library binding)
ISBN: 978-1-62065-743-0 (paperback)
ISBN: 978-1-4765-1094-1 (eBook PDF)

Editorial Credits
Jeni Wittrock, editor; Bobbie Nuytten, designer; Svetlana Zhurkin, media researcher;
Jennifer Walker, production specialist

Photo Credits
Dreamstime: Denise Lett, 16–17; Shutterstock: Alex Staroseltsev, 1 (top), alterfalter, cover (left), Artur
Synenko, 4–5, auremar, 20–21, Benjamin Haas, 8–9, c. (cardboard texture), cover (top), Danny E. Hooks, 6–7,
GMEVIPHOTO, 28 (beans), Julian Rovagnati, 2–3, limpido, cover (right), 1 (right), Maxim Kalmykov, 10–11,
Moreno Soppelsa, 28 (back), 30, 31, 32, Nikola Bilic, 28 (tape), pashabo (recycled paper texture), cover and
throughout, Picsfive, 14–15, Richard Thornton, 18–19, Robbi, 28 (bottle), Semen Lixodeev, 12–13, stoonn, 24–25,
Ulrich Mueller, 22–23, Vitaly Korovin, 28 (markers), worradirek, 26–27; Svetlana Zhurkin, 29

Note to Parents, Teachers, and Librarians
This Earth Matters book uses full color photographs and a nonfiction format to introduce the concept
of earth science and is designed to be read aloud to a pre-reader or to be read independently by an
early reader. Photographs help listeners and early readers understand the text and concepts discussed.
The book encourages further learning by including the following sections: Glossary, Read More,
Internet Sites, and Index. Early readers may need assistance using these features.

Printed in the United States of America in North Mankato, Minnesota.
092012   006933CGS13